SOFT
deliveries

SOFT
deliveries

A 'century' of yarns
selected by
RICHARD HADLEE

REED

Published by Reed Books, a division of Reed Publishing (NZ) Ltd, 39 Rawene Rd, Birkenhead, Auckland. Associated companies, branches and representatives throughout the world.

ISBN 0 7900 0505 0

First published 1996

Designed by Clair Stutton
Illustrations by K.S. Clark
Printed by Wright and Carman (NZ) Limited, Wellington

To all the cricketers I've met and the
characters the game produces.

contents

An opening word	11
Biography	12

THE COMMENTATORS — 13

The power of radio	15
I'm sorry, I'll read that again	18
Memorable moments	20
What they really said	21
Brian's blob	22
The longest time	23

THE CHARACTERS — 25

Nicknames	27
Ted of the terraces	28
Jock the keeper	29
Stimpo the bowler	30
Surrender	32
The best of Boock	33
John Wright	35
A testing time	37
Short on brains?	38
Slow and steady	39

CANTERBURY — 41

Horse McNally's natural game	41
Practice makes imperfect	42

NEW ZEALAND — 43

Question and answer	45
Practice? We've had ours	47
Tickets on tour	48
Dayle meets the Queen	49

ENGLAND — 51

Honoured to sign	53
Stumped	55
A clear view	56
How fast?	57
Lords knows	58
Not on a full stomach	59
A sour note	60
The earth moves	61
Yes, my lord	62
The great Boycott	63

WEST INDIES — 65

Rolling on	67
No-balls	68
The chosen one	69
Call me Amby	70
Lara rules	71
Wally prepares	72
Optimism	73

INDIA AND PAKISTAN — 75

Blowin' in the wind	77
Audience participation	78
Which way is the pitch?	79

Doctor's orders	80	HISTORY	113
Spare seat	81	Strange but true	115
The missing wallet	82	Cricket was once played on	
Early bird	84	horseback	116
Everything's all right	85	All over	117
AUSTRALIA	87	IT HAPPENED TO ME	119
Saved!	89	A bowler's graveyard	121
Pascoe's promise	90	Gotcha!	122
Bouncers	91	Humour for Hadlee	124
Much too appealing	92	Who are you?	125
Amended rules of play	93	In black and white	126
		Bowled over	128
SOUTH AFRICA	95	From sir to sir	129
Heads or tails	97	Who needs a bat?	130
Down to size	98	Fast, faster, fastest	131
Ship ahoy	99	In at the death	132
Diving for cover	100	Directions	133
		All the best to Border	134
NOTTINGHAM	101		
Derek Randall	103	EXTRAS	137
Hendrick's humour	107	The Bobbitt delivery	139
The right thing to say	108	Batting in a crisis	140
A matter of pace	109	Hit on the Paddy	141
Seeing the light	110	Short and to the point	142
Keith Pont travels	111	All in a day's play	143
in the outfield		Get off the grass	144
No ball, no laughing matter	112	You can bank on it	145
		Too much hot air?	146
		Who nose what to do	147

A dog's tale   148
Leave it to Liz   149
Just five more   150
Happy to go   151
Members   152
A call from above   153
The unkindest cut of all   154
How big?   155
An important announcement 156
How many balls?   157
Caught out   158
Champagne all round   159
Well fielded   160

an opening word

Over my many years in cricket, I've recorded a multitude of amusing and interesting stories about the game and its long history — the people who play it, the overseas tours, the commentators, the humorous things that have happened to me and to others. This light-hearted look at the game is the result. Nothing in these pages is intended to demean or offend anyone. The aim of these stories is to provide a good laugh. I hope you will enjoy reading them as much as I have enjoyed collecting them.

Richard Hadlee

biography

Richard Hadlee, born in Christchurch in 1951, played cricket for Canterbury 1971-90, Tasmania 1979-80, Nottinghamshire 1978-87 and New Zealand 1972-90. In 1981 he was awarded an MBE for services to New Zealand sport and in 1990 a knighthood for services to cricket. He was named New Zealand Sportsman of the Year in 1980 and 1986, New Zealand Sportsperson of the Last 25 Years in 1987 and New Zealand Sportsperson of the Decade in 1989.

He played 86 test matches and 115 one-day internationals and captured 431 test wickets (a world record until it was surpassed by Kapil Dev). His best bowling performance was nine for 52 against Australia at the Gabba in 1985-86. He scored 3124 test runs at an average of 27.16; his highest test score was 151 not out against Sri Lanka.

On 4 February 1990, on his home ground of Lancaster Park in Christchurch Richard Hadlee became the first bowler in test history to capture 400 test wickets. The great Sir Don Bradman once described him as 'the master of rhythm and swing'.

the COMMENTATORS

the power *of* radio

His 'accidental' spoonerisms — 'And it's Masif Asood (Asif Masood) from the pavilion end!'— and double meanings — 'The bowler's Holding, the batsman's Willey' — have contributed heavily to Brian Johnston's cult following.

Johnston's other character traits, such as his practical jokes and the cavalier bestowing of nicknames — for example, I was always Hadders — made Johnners a major menace. Usually, he was in full control but on occasions he lost it totally, breaking into uncontrollable fits of laughter.

Some years ago, after the second day's play in the fifth test at the Oval, Brian Johnston was discussing the day's events on air with John Agnew. After an absence of 20 tests, it was inevitable that Ian Botham's innings and unusual dismissal (hit wicket) should command attention. Having described exactly how 'the legend's' pad had removed a bail, the BBC's cricket correspondent completed his summary of the event by stating that Botham had been unable 'to get his leg over'.

It was a remark made in all innocence, but it resulted in a sharp intake of breath from the other (silent) occupants of the box (producer Peter Baxter and Tony Cozier). Johnners, who got the giggles, tried to carry on with the scoreboard, pausing only for the occasional, 'Stop it, Aggers!'

When he caught sight of the others in the box, with tears of laughter streaming down their cheeks, his voice took on a higher pitch and his reading of the scoreboard soon resembled the famous Michael Bentine rendition of the soccer results. The climax of his performance was a 23-second silence.

This incident was heard by thousands of listeners and featured in the following day's tabloids. A letter was received from a motorist who, along with many other motorists, had heard the broadcast while driving through the Dartford Tunnel, and was caught up in the ensuing traffic jam which tailed back for 3 miles.

Another calamity had occurred in Milton Keynes, but news of it did not reach the test match special commentary team until the Nat West Final, when they received, from the BBC's head of litigation, a copy of a letter from solicitor Tony Alexander. The letter read:

We have been consulted by Mr Wally Painter and his wife Dolly. On Friday evening, our clients were in the process of redecorating the hallway. Mr Painter was perched on a ladder in the stairwell of his house whilst Mrs Painter held the ladder steady. Our client's aquarium, with assorted tropical fish, was situated at the foot of the stairwell.

Our clients, who are keen cricket enthusiasts, were listening to the summary of the day's play on Radio 3, when Mr Brian Johnston and Mr John Agnew were discussing Mr Ian Botham's dismissal, which apparently involved some footwork which Mr Botham failed to consummate.

The ensuing events caused a vibration in the ladder and, in spite of Mrs Painter's firm grasp, Mr Painter fell off the ladder, landing awkwardly on the landing and thereby dislocating his wrist. The ladder fell on Mrs Painter, who suffered a contusion to her forehead. The 5-litre drum of Dulux Sandalwood emulsion fell and crashed through the aquarium which flooded the hallway, depositing various frantically flapping exotic fish onto a Persian rug. The Painters' pedigree Persian cat (Mr Painter spent many years in Teheran as an adviser to the Shah) grabbed one of the fish, a Malayan red-spined gurnot, and simply choked to death.

The water seeped down into the cellar where the electricity meters were located. There were several short circuits which resulted in (a) the main switchboard being severely damaged and (b) the burglar alarm (which was connected to the local police) being set off.

Meanwhile, Mr and Mrs Painter were staggering towards the bathroom, apparently in paroxysms of hysterical laughter despite their injuries. Within minutes, the police arrived and, believing the Painters to be vandals and suspecting, as both were incoherent, that they had been taking drugs, promptly arrested them.

We are now instructed to inform you that our clients hold the corporation [BBC] liable for:

(a) Their personal injuries

(b) Loss of the aquarium and various exotic fish

(c) Damage to the Persian rug

(d) Death of the cat.

However, they are prepared to settle all claims for damages in respect of the above, providing that you supply them with a recording of the discussion between Mr Johnston and Mr Agnew, together with an undertaking from Mr Johnston and Mr Agnew that they will not in future discuss Mr Botham's footwork, or lack of it, while Mr and Mrs Painter are decorating their property.

I am happy to report that Mr and Mrs Painter received their tape.

I'm sorry, *I'll* read that again

Cricket commentators can make a game marvellously vivid for radio listeners, but some broadcasters have ended up with very red faces when they've made a mistake or realised the second meanings of some of their comments.

'Welcome to Leicester, where Ray Illingworth has just relieved himself at the pavilion end.'

'Barry Richards, the great South African batsman, has just hit one of Basil D'Olivera's balls clean out of the ground.'

'Boycott has advanced down the pitch, opening his legs and showing us his class.'

'Kallicharan has just had a slash outside off stump.'

'Norman O'Neill is fielding in the leg slip position, legs wide apart, waiting for a tickle.'

'The batsman has chanced his arm and it's come off.'

The BBC newsreader reading out the cricket results: 'Yorkshire, all out for 364, Hutton out ill. I'm sorry, I'll read that again. Hutton out, 111.'

'Hadlee is a bowler who can bounce his balls past the batsman's nose.'

'Geoff Howarth has played the ball through the on side for two runs. That was a fine shit — ah, I mean fine shot.'

Ian Chappell, the former Australian captain, had a habit of hitching his box after he had played a shot at the ball. The TV camera moved in, but the commentator wasn't watching the screen when he said, 'Well, it's been a good pitch. Only two balls have moved all day.'

'John Emburey, the English off-spinner, is bowling with two short legs and one of them is wearing a helmet.'

During the 1960 test match between England and West Indies at Sabina Park in Jamaica, the commentator said, 'Well, it's a nice day here at Sabina Park. The wind is shining and the sun is blowing gently across the ground.'

Arthur Morris had played well for Australia during the day except that he had dropped England's batsman Jack Crapp or, as the commentator said, 'Morris has had a good day, but he has had one blemish. He dropped Crapp in the outfield.'

Rex Alston was commentating on a match at Lords. 'No runs scored from that over bowled by Jack Young, which means that he has had four maidens on the trot.'

The first test against the West Indies in Dunedin in 1980 was an incredible game. We played well enough to win the game by at least five wickets, but we managed to creep home by just one wicket. The Windies batted first and made 140. We replied with 249. At 108 for four, in the Windies' second innings, Collis King hit a four to take them to 112 for four, which meant they had wiped out the deficit, or, as Peter Williams the TV commentator said, 'They are now back in the black.'

memorable moments

A commentator was trying to distinguish between two players during a World Series Cricket match in which South African Clive Rice was batting with West Indian Collis King. He said, 'Rice is the batsman under the white helmet and King is the batsman with the black and curly helmet.'

My brother Dayle, who was having an off day, was bowling quite poorly to Middlesex and England's No. 3 batsman, Clive Radley. 'And sadly,' listeners heard, 'Hadlee bowls badly to Radley.'

Syed Kirmani, the Indian wicketkeeper, was having a great deal of difficulty keeping to Bishen Bedi on a turning pitch. He conceded several byes and the next time he missed the ball the commentator said, 'Bedi byes.'

Fred Trueman describing Jerry Coney, a gentle, medium pace bowler, said, 'Coney runs in to bowl, rather, he walks into bowl. He has bowled the ball so slowly, that by the time the ball reaches the other end the batsman has played himself out of form.'

'Surrey started cautiously and only three runs were scored in the first hour's play. Clarke was the more aggressive of the two batsmen.'

New Zealand were playing England and both Jeff and Martin Crowe had a disappointing match. Umpire Harold, Dickie, Bird had to make a decision or, as the commentator said, 'At the Oval test 1983, both Crowes scored ducks and one was given out by a bird.'

what they *really* said

Commentators make a lot of assumptions, simply because they are not as close to the playing situations as the players. A case in point was when Keith Miller was captaining a team that included Peter Philpott. As the team walked onto the field, Miller turned to his players and the commentator assumed that he was giving them a last- minute team talk. According to Peter Philpott, what he had said was, 'Scatter, you bastards!'

And on another occasion New Zealand captain Jeremy Coney, who was fielding at second slip, walked over to wicketkeeper Ian Smith.

'He's asking Smith for advice,' the commentator told his listeners. 'There's no doubt at all that Coney wants to know whether Hadlee's outswinger is moving enough in the air to cause the batsmen problems. A third slip will be needed for a possible catch in that area.'

Jerry had asked Ian Smith for advice, but Smithy's reply was, 'Look, Jerry, slow left at 4 o'clock: girl on boundary edge wearing red knickers.'

brian's *blob*

Brian Johnston, the great English commentator, was also a cricketer in his own right. When he was playing for the Lord's Taverners Club, at the end of the day's play, his dog, Blob, would walk onto the field, pick up Brian's wicketkeeping gloves and waddle back to the pavilion. Other members of the team very quickly nicknamed Blob Larwood, after the great fast bowler Harold Larwood, because he had four short legs and his balls swung both ways.

the longest time

In January 1996, Robert Kennedy, a young fast bowler who had made a meteoric rise in international cricket, was playing in only his second ODI, against Zimbabwe at McLean Park in Napier. He had one of those indifferent bowling spells with frequent wides and no-balls. In total, he bowled about 12 wides and three no-balls in his nine-over spell. The commentators were not slow to take advantage of his misfortune.

John Wright: 'Robert Kennedy is having some difficulty with his line out there. It's going to be a long over — let's hope he completes it before the lights come on!' (It was then 3.10 p.m.; the lights were due to come on at 6.45.)

Grant Nesbitt turned to me and said, between balls, 'I've got a race to listen to.' When I asked what time it started, he replied, 'In about 20 minutes, but with the way he's bowling at the moment, I'm likely to miss it.'

I was guilty too. At our hospitality function during the tea break, I welcomed our guests and added, 'We've received a late apology from Robert Kennedy. He's still trying to complete one of his overs.'

the CHARACTERS

nicknames

The origins of cricketers' nicknames can be quite interesting.

John Wright was known as Shake because he used to lift the lid of his cricket case, throw his clothes in, close the lid and then shake the case until everything fitted.

Richard Collinge was called Rock because his initials were ROC, and Bruce Murray was Bags because his initials were BAG.

Lance Cairns was Springers because he used to play his cricket in Blenheim, for a team called Spring Creek.

Jerry Coney was Mantis because, at times, he ran like a praying mantis.

Chris Old, Yorkshire and England fast bowler, became Chilly because he was C. Old.

Derek Underwood was christened Deadly for his accurate and lethal bowling on pitches that suited him.

Derek Randall was Arkle or Rags. He was so athletic and fast in the outfield that he was nicknamed Arkle after a thoroughbred horse. Rags came from his school days when his clothes were a little tatty.

Mike Harris, who played for Nottingham during the 1970s and early 1980s was Pasty, because he came from Cornwall, well known for its pasties.

Jeff Crowe became Chopper because of his axeman's shoulders and his brother Martin was Hogan because, as a boy, he captained a team named after the TV programme Hogan's Heroes.

Tony Blain was known as Chill or Chilblain, for obvious reasons.

ted *of the* terraces

One of the unsung heroes and characters of Eden Park is Lord Ted — the King of the Terraces. He is there for every test match and, when the sun is out, he parades around bare-chested. Every time he starts to walk around the terraces, usually well packed with spectators, shouts of 'Sit down, Ted!' can be clearly heard. He also has the habit of chatting up women in the crowd and he causes a lot of amusement and entertainment.

The TV cameras happened to focus in on Lord Ted as he went on one of his walks around the terraces. As Ted's statistics flashed across the screen, Peter Williams, the TV commentator, said, 'And there is Lord Ted, King of the Terraces. Fifty test appearances, 2000 cans at an average of 40 cans per test. His best performance, 18 cans in a day.'

(It should be noted that these statistics include rain-affected test matches. It is also understood that Lord Ted is opposed to test matches without rest days!)

jock *the* keeper

Jock Edwards went to England in 1978 as New Zealand's No. 1 keeper. Jock would admit that he had a difficult time in many ways, mainly because he was known more as a batsman than as a keeper. There's no doubt in my mind that keeping wickets probably affected his batting on tour and that was a shame for us.

During the second test against England at Trentbridge, Jock had let through several byes, dropped the odd catch and also misfielded several return throws from the outfield. His performance probably left a lot to be desired.

Trevor Bailey, the commentator, said, 'If Jock Edwards went to the North Pole, he wouldn't catch a cold!'

In 1975, New Zealand competed against Western Australia at the MCG to win the Australasian One Day Competition.

WA were in awful trouble at 28 for seven, but they managed to score 80 odd.

New Zealand opened with Jock Edwards, a short stocky young man who liked to hit the ball, especially hooking and cutting. Dennis Lillee opened the bowling for WA and Jocko, full of try, accepted the challenge and hooked Lillee for a couple of fours, one of them going over the head of wicketkeeper Rod Marsh.

Lillee said to Jock, 'Where did you learn to hook, sonny?'

Jock replied, 'I'm learning as I go, sir!'

stimpo *the* bowler

Fast bowler Alan Stimpson, Stimpo, was playing for Northern Districts against Canterbury in a Plunket Shield match. While Stimpo was batting, the square leg umpire decided to stand at point to get a better view, as the sun restricted his view from the square leg position.

It's normal procedure for the umpire to advise the batsman where he intends to stand, so he said, 'Batsman, I'm standing on the off side.' There was no reply, so the umpire repeated himself twice more. Again there was no reply and the Canterbury captain, Maurice Ryan, said, 'Stimpo, I think he's talking to you.'

Stimpo said, 'I'm no batsman, I'm a bowler!'

Stimpo always fancied himself to score a 100 but he knew the only way he could get his chance was to volunteer for the nightwatch-man's job. Batting at 11 didn't give him a great opportunity to fulfil his dream. His chance came, and, at 5.55 p.m. he was in and played out two overs until 6 p.m. without difficulty.

He then proceeded to do all the things that not-out batsmen should do: an early night, down at the ground early next morning to have an hour of throwdowns, a shower and some imaginary practice shots in the dressing room before going out to bat at 11 a.m., looking a million dollars.

With the first ball of the morning, Stimpo played defensively forward and gently nicked the ball to the keeper to be out caught behind. He stood his ground because he couldn't believe his eyes. It almost needed a crane to pull him off the field after the umpire's finger was raised.

Once, while Stimpo was waiting to go in to bat, he started to read a book. He was interrupted by his captain, who gave him some words of advice on how to play the bowling and what he was required to do. The wicket fell and Stimpo walked boldly to the crease and proceeded to play defensively, obviously under instructions.

He pushed forward, the ball hitting the pad and falling in front of him. The close in fielder picked up the ball and also the book that Stimpo had been reading, which he had put inside the top of his pad. The title? How to Play Golf.

surrender

Dennis Amiss and Tony Greig completely dominated England's second innings during the first test at Trentbridge, Nottingham in 1973. England made 250 and New Zealand 97. In their second innings England were a remarkable 24 for four, until Amiss and Greig both cut loose with 138 and 139 respectively.

When Amiss scored his 100, he tore into Bruce Taylor's seamers, sending four consecutive balls crashing to the boundary, all perfectly executed shots. Before Taylor bowled his fifth ball, he produced a white handkerchief from his pocket and waved it in the air to show that he had surrendered.

A similar thing happened in a World Series Cricket ODI between New Zealand and India at Brisbane in 1981. Kapil Dev launched into Jerry Coney's dribblies, hitting him for two consecutive sixes into the Clem Jones Stand.

The white hanky was produced, much to the displeasure of Ian Taylor, our manager, and Frank Cameron, chairman of selectors and assistant tour manager. (The end result, Coney, 10 overs, no wicket for 70.)

the best *of* Boock

Stephen Boock was a great character, always looking for situations to create interest and amusement and perhaps even help his own game. He believed in targets and, like me, he had inspiring words on the inside of his cricket coffin lid, to remind him of what he should do.

My card reads, 'Motivation — a quitter never wins and a winner never quits. Believe in yourself, beat your opponent, enjoy the game, remain focused and be happy with your performance, even if somebody does better. Give it your best shot.' In Boocky's lid the card says, 'SHUT THIS CASE!'

He did, however, have goals for the 1990 season and for his career: 1) to capture a further 326 test wickets to be the first bowler to reach 400 test wickets (he had only 74 at the time); 2) to score 193 more test runs to achieve the coveted double — 400 test wickets and 400 test runs; 3) to swim Cook Strait underwater; and 4) to be the subject of 'This Is Your Life' before Richard Hadlee.

Unfortunately Stephen did not realise any of his goals during his career. He was 326 test wickets short, 193 runs short of 400, he failed to turn up for the swim and the organisers of 'This is Your Life' had never heard of him.

Stephen Boock holds a New Zealand bowling record that he would probably rather forget.

In 1988, New Zealand were playing Pakistan at Eden Park on a pitch that was an absolute belter. The batsmen were having a wonderful time. I had Mudassar Nazar out early but Miandad (271), Shaoib (112), Malik (80) and Imran (60 not out) were enjoying their time at the crease.

It was at this time that I ruptured my Achilles tendon, which put me out of the game and the rest of the series. My figures of one for 74 certainly weren't impressive and now the bowling had to be shared among the other bowlers.

Boocky had to bear the brunt of the bowling responsibilities and he ended up bowling a marathon spell of 74 overs and took one for 229. To concede three runs per over was a great effort, but he ended up in the record book for conceding the most runs in an innings by a New Zealand bowler.

As his 200 runs came up on the scoreboard, the crowd sympathetically applauded the milestone in his career. Imran Khan, the Pakistan captain, smiling, also congratulated him. Boocky, seeing the funny side of the situation, proceeded to kneel on the pitch and kiss the turf — all with great dignity and pride.

The over ended without further runs being scored and Boocky walked rather slowly to fine leg. Then, just as Ewen Chatfield started his run-up a loud voice called, 'Hey Charlie, I've left some moisture on the pitch. See if you can use it to your advantage!'

At that stage, Pakistan were 580 for five but Charlie obviously wasn't able to follow Boocky's advice. Pakistan ended up with 640 for six declared.

In the 1978-79 season Otago travelled to Christchurch for their match against Canterbury. Boocky had been having trouble with his batting grip so he thought he'd do something about it. He glued his batting gloves to the handle of the bat in approximately the correct position before walking out to bat, holding the bat in both hands.

He went in as night watchman and survived.

The next day, as he continued his innings, his hands became a little sweaty. Needing to change his gloves, he held up his bat with both gloves dangling from the handle and, sure enough, the 12th man brought out a fresh pair. He scored 23.

john wright

Shake Wright had to wait 16 tests before he scored his maiden test century, which was against the Indians at Eden Park, Auckland, in 1981. Before that, Shake would have been the first to admit that his test performances were only satisfactory. At times he had experienced bad luck and he felt that his 'bat was lacking in confidence'. When he met New Zealand Prime Minister Rob Muldoon, he asked him to sign his bat, hoping that it would give it more punch and flair, because he was sick of labouring in the middle!

John Wright was rooming with Gary Troup in Wellington before the third and final ODI match against Australia in 1982. Troupy woke up at 7 a.m. to see Shake sneaking around the room with a rolled-up newspaper in his hand. He looked behind the curtains and then opened the outside door and went out into the rain. Coming back in, he said, 'Where the hell is that bloody cricket?' He then went over to his briefcase and opened it and said, 'Oh no!' He had found the so-called cricket. The noise he had heard was the alarm on his wristwatch.

John Wright and Jerry Coney were always having little bets with each other and doing crazy things. At one stage they had a dare with each other. Shake had to find a telephone box in a main street, sit on top of it and use his shoe as the telephone. Passers-by looked up in amazement, thinking they had seen a new Maxwell Smart! Mantis, on the other hand, had to turn up to the nets on the back ground of Eden Park during a test match dressed in his white shirt, New Zealand tie, blazer and cap, with white trousers and black shoes. He bowled in the nets with the test match gallery viewing proceedings. It really was a funny sight.

At a team selection meeting we were discussing the vacant batting position and the two or three players who were vying for it.

Shake said, 'Jeff Crowe has been batting brilliantly, so he's got to play. I haven't seen him bat as yet.' He had to pause for about 20 seconds as the rest of us broke into laughter before he continued with, 'Anyway, he told me that he was batting well!'

John Wright, New Zealand's leading run scorer with over 5000 runs, will remember his last test innings but probably for the wrong reasons. He scored a solid 30-odd which helped New Zealand beat Australia in 1993 at Eden Park and square the series one all.

What John will remember is that he was the first New Zealand batsman to be given out in a test by the third umpire — a TV replay. He had been going for a quick single when the wicket was broken. Umpire Brian Aldridge signalled for the replay and Wrighty stood in the middle waiting for the decision from the replay. He was out by centimetres and off he headed towards the pavilion as the red light indicated that the decision had gone against him.

At the after-match press conference Wrighty was interviewed about his retirement, the last match and, of course, his last innings in test cricket. John has a dry sense of humour and when it came to talking about his dismissal, he said, 'At the end of the match, the umpires came into the dressing room and presented me with a certificate saying the third umpire said, "You were out!" It was just like receiving a traffic ticket, except this time I wasn't done for speeding.'

a testing time

John Bracewell hadn't played a lot of first-class cricket when he was selected for the 1980-81 tour of Australia. He played in the first test against Australia at Brisbane, which was a disaster for New Zealand, with the Australians convincingly winning the five-day match in three days.

The quote of the tour was found when someone asked Braces what he thought of playing test cricket. 'It's just like playing any other three-day match,' said John.

Short *on* brains?

Derek, Billy, Stirling was a young New Zealand fast bowler who toured Sri Lanka in 1984. It is said that fast bowlers are a little like front row props in rugby — rather short on brains. This is most unfair; we fast bowlers can complete a two-piece jigsaw puzzle in five minutes.

When Billy was doing some shopping in Colombo, he asked the price of some shorts.

'300 rupees,' was the reply.

'Oh, too dear,' said Billy. 'But how much is the shirt?'

'300 rupees.'

'Too dear,' said Billy. 'How much for them both?'

'600 rupees,' said the salesman.

'Okay,' said Billy. 'I'll take them both.'

slow *and* steady

Ewen Chatfield was a great foil for me over my career. He bowled a magnificent, very consistent line and length to tie the one end down, while I could be more attacking from the other. Charlie was a wonderful servant for Wellington and New Zealand cricket, always giving 100 per cent. During one match, Charlie bowled 30 overs in the day, a wonderful effort.

In the early days, his fielding was somewhat ungainly and awkward, but as time went on he became more competent and was very useful. I well remember the two catches he took at deep fine leg, off my bowling, to dismiss the 'Happy Hooker', Andrew Hilditch, at the Gabba in 1985.

While not bowling he was always positioned at fine leg or third man to rest. In fact whenever the ball came his way he moved rather sheepishly and slowly. Somehow, once, a tortoise crawled onto the field of play during a match. Charlie looked at the tortoise and said, 'Piss off you, little bastard. You've been following me around all day!'

CANTERBURY

horse mcnally's natural game

Canterbury were 230 for eight in the first innings against Otago during the 1981-82 season. We had 25 of the mandatory 100 overs left in which to score the 20 runs we needed to get another bonus point.

Cran Bull, the captain, told Steve McNally, our No. 10 batsman, to take it easy as there was plenty of time and we needed more runs for an important batting point. Steve, or Horse as he is known, strode to the wicket and missed the first ball, bowled by off-spinner John Bracewell. He skied the next ball straight up into the air and was caught by the fielder in the bat/pad position.

In such a hurry to get off the field that he was nearly at a canter, he had to pass the captain, who said, 'What do you think you are playing at?'

Horse replied, 'I thought I'd play my natural game.' He was obviously disappointed and very angry with himself.

By the end of the day things had settled down and the lads started to take the mickey out of him in the dressing room.

'Was the ball turning, Horse?' 'You didn't seem to play the spin bowler that well!' 'You were a little unlucky to get caught bat/pad the way you played that shot!'

In the second innings, he played his natural game again. He was out for two, caught in the deep off the same bowler. Some people, I guess, only learn the hard way.

practice *makes* imperfect

Canterbury were playing Otago at Carisbrook during the 1981-82 season. Canterbury scrambled for 243 while Otago were all out for 164. Stephen Boock was out second ball for no score. The game took a dramatic turn when we were 117 for three in the second innings. John Bracewell came on to bowl, taking seven for 9, and Canterbury were all out for 124. Otago were well placed at stumps, needing only 137 with eight wickets to win the match.

Boock was having his normal throwdowns the next morning, obviously anticipating having to bat. I couldn't help noticing his attacking of the ball, which he was hitting with great power over the bowler's head to several fielders in the deep. This was something I had never seen from Boocky.

Otago duly got the runs, winning the game by seven wickets. At the end of the game, I asked Boocky, who hadn't been required to bat, about his batting practice. He said, 'I was practising having a quick slog for nought!'

NEW ZEALAND

question *and* answer

During their careers, players are asked to do many different things including signing autographs, appearing at promotional functions, visiting hospitals — and filling in questionnaires about their life. Some players take full advantage of this situation to entertain readers with amusing and sometimes outrageous responses.

Take the 1993-94 New Zealand team, for example.

1. What is the best advice your mother gave you?

Tony Blain: 'Never marry a nymphomaniac because the honeymoon is great but after that it's hard work.'

Ken Rutherford: 'Abstain from alcohol — I didn't listen.'

Shane Thomson: 'Not to hook in the first over. (My most embarrassing moment — hooking and getting caught out in the first over.)'

2. What is your earliest memory?

Mark Greatbatch: 'The nurse slapping me.'

Adam Parore: 'Running around stark naked, covered in finger paint, wearing a blue cape and pretending to be superman — I was 17! Just kidding — I was three.'

Chris Pringle: 'Getting hit on the head with a golf club, aged three.'

Ken Rutherford: 'Cutting my umbilical cord.'

Bryan Young: 'Nearly being run over while in a pushchair.'

3. What would you hate to be without in life?

Matthew Hart: 'My box when facing the West Indies pace attack.'

4. What is your most embarrassing moment?

Mark Haslam: 'The first three balls I bowled for New Zealand against Zimbabwe B. They all went for four.'

Danny Morrison: 'Breaking wind on Donna's physio table and her saying, "There are only two of us here and Danny, you can't blame the stuffed panda bear in the corner!"'

Chris Pringle: 'Going out to bat in Pakistan with two right-handed gloves.'

Willie Watson: 'Every time I open my mouth.'

Jeff Wilson: 'Sitting in Martin Crowe's seat in the New Zealand dressing room.'

5. What is the best thing about being a cricketer?

Andrew Jones: 'Scoring runs. (The worst thing is having to field).'

6. What is the worst thing about being a cricketer?

Dion Nash: 'A forearm and vee-neck suntan.'

Willie Watson: 'Watching yourself bowling in the television high-lights and everything goes for four or six. Also, bowling in the "happy hour" in a one-day match [the last few overs] and again, everything goes for four or six.'

7. What is your ambition in life?

Adam Parore: 'To go on tour where my phone bill is less than $1,000.'

Practice? We've had ours

We had beaten Aussie in the first final of the best of five series at Sydney under floodlights. It was a very good win and gave us a big advantage in the series. Next day, both teams travelled to Melbourne on the same plane. The Aussie manager, John Edwards, asked Tails if we were going to practise in Melbourne.

It was a question that needed answering because both teams could not practise at the MCG at the same time. 'Practice!' said Tails. 'We had ours last night!' It was a magnificent comment, but it soon turned sour because the Aussies won the next three games to win the series three to one.

tickets *on* tour

Ian Taylor was a wonderful manager on tour. He always had the players' interests at heart, but at the same time he had to be responsible to the New Zealand Cricket Council Board members. He also had a sense of humour that at times took players unawares.

It is traditional for all players to receive complimentary match tickets for family and friends to come and watch the games. On the tour of Australia in 1980-81, I said to Tails, 'Boss, I'd like my two complimentary tickets for the test.'

'Why do you want two tickets, Paddles?' he asked.

'For my Mum and Dad, boss,' I replied.

'Listen here, Paddles,' he said. 'If your Mum and Dad won't pay to see you play, how can you expect others to pay to watch you play?'

What answer could I give to that theory?

dayle *meets the* queen

When meeting royalty, a certain level of etiquette is expected. Generally, the players are briefed before the meeting to avoid any possible embarrassment. In 1969, the New Zealand cricket team was introduced to the Queen at Lords. My brother Dayle proudly shook hands and said, 'Nice to meet you. How's your son?'

'Which son do you mean?' the Queen asked.

'I only know one,' Dayle replied.

In 1978, at Buckingham Palace, Dayle met the Queen again. In trying to make polite conversation, he asked, 'How is Princess Anne's horse riding getting on?'

The Queen replied, 'You mean her show jumping?'

On another occasion, he was reported as saying, 'And what does your daughter do for a crust?'

ENGLAND

honoured *to* sign

Our first game of the 1983 tour of England was a two-day match against the Combined Services team at Portsmouth. After the first day's play, both teams attended a dinner function at HMS Nelson. On our arrival we had to sign the visitors' book. Everything was very formal and precise, as is normally the case where great tradition is involved.

Our manager, Sir Allan Wright, signed the book first, followed by Geoff Howarth and me. The entries read as follows:

Sir Allan Wright KBE (manager, New Zealand cricket team)
Geoff Howarth MBE (captain of New Zealand cricket team)
Richard Hadlee MBE (player New Zealand cricket team).

After reading these first three entries, the other players duly signed the book:
John Wright IPG (I play guitar)
John Bracewell GD (grave digger)
Ian Smith WKB (wicketkeeper, batsman)
Martin Snedden LALOB (left arm, lower order batsman)
Trevor Franklin HM (Herman Munster)
Lance Cairns AFFCO (Auckland Farmers' Freezing Company)
 Martin Crowe BCMFOS (Bachelor of Cosmetics & Max Factor Old Spice)
Jeff Crowe MBE (my brother's efforts)
Bruce Edgar BCA (Bachelor of Commerce and Administration)
Wally Lees TTC (Trained Teacher's Certificate)
Ewen Chatfield Dip. Ag., ICB (Diploma of Agriculture, I can't bat)

Jerry Coney BA, Dip. T., RMFB, MOB (Bachelor of Arts, Diploma of Teaching, right arm medium fast bowler, middle order batsman)

Peter Borrie MD, FRACP (Doctor of Medicine, Fellow of the Royal Australasian College of Physicians)

John Joseph Patrick O'Sullivan OEC (One-eyed Cantabrian, scorer, New Zealand cricket team).

stumped

In 1983, New Zealand were playing the second test against England at Trentbridge. I was bowling to Phil Edmonds, who batted at No. 8 for England. His nickname is Rommel because he disagrees with anything and everything to do with cricket.

Just as I started to bowl, he said, 'Umpire, would you ask the bowler to remove his wrist bands? They're upsetting my concentration.'

'He's taking the piss,' I said to umpire Kenny Palmer. 'It's the first time in my career that I've been asked to remove my wrist bands!'

'Get them off,' said Kenny.

I guess it was a polite enough request but I wasn't happy with the situation because the batsman now had an edge over me. I had time to think about this while the next over was in progress. At the start of my over, I went up to Kenny and said, 'Would you mind asking the batsman to remove his helmet? It's upsetting my concentration and I can't see the whites of his eyes.'

'Stop taking the piss and get on with the game,' was Kenny's reply.

The game continued and we needed 137 runs in the second innings to win the match. Edmonds bowled (slow, left arm spin) with his Swatch on. No doubt he was paid some good money to promote the product. Jeremy Coney was batting with Martin Crowe.

Crowe said to umpire Palmer, 'Would you mind asking the bowler to remove his watch?'

The watch was duly removed, Crowe took a single and Coney was now on strike.

'Umpire,' said Coney. 'Would you please ask the bowler to put his watch back on again?'

To see Edmonds stumped for words was an absolute delight.

a *clear* view

On the New Zealand 1994 tour of England, the traditional MCC dinner was held at Lords. Matthew Hart, New Zealand's 21-year-old left arm spin bowler, was sitting beside Tony Lewis, a former captain of England and now a television commentator with the BBC.

The Long Room at Lords is a wonderful venue at any time, but especially for a banquet dinner. Harty kept looking out of the windows, shaking his head from time to time.

Tony asked Matthew if this was his first time at Lords.

'No, I know this ground very well because I was on the ground staff here three years ago.'

'These windows give a terrific view of the ground, Matthew,' said Tony. 'Soon you'll be walking out of the Long Room onto the hallowed turf with your bat in hand and one day you will bowl your slow left arm spin from the members' end. Did you ever imagine then that one day you'd be doing that for your country?'

'Not at all!' Matthew replied. 'I was too busy cleaning all these flipping windows!'

how fast?

When travelling down the M1 in England, Fred Trueman was pulled over for speeding. The policeman, who obviously recognised his victim, said, 'Ah, Mr Trueman, are you trying to drive as fast as you bowl?'

Fred replied, 'Now listen here, sunshine, if I was doing that, you'd never have caught me!'

He was let off the speeding fine for originality.

lords knows

During the late 1960s former English player and selector Doug Insole received a letter from an irate supporter who thought he could do a better job in team selection because he knew more about the game than Insole did.

The letter Insole received had been re-directed because it had been addressed to: Mr Doug Insole, c/o Lords, Westminster, London.

The letter, which was re-addressed to Mr Doug Insole, c/o Lords, St Johns Wood, London, contained a covering letter saying, 'Dear Sir, I'm enclosing this letter which I'm sure you can answer far better than we can at the House of Lords. We have therefore sent this letter to you at Lords Cricket Ground. Yours faithfully, Minister of Internal Affairs.'

not on a *full* stomach

As captain you must deal with many problems, both on and off the field, but when your fast bowler fails to turn up, there's nothing you can do. A Transvaal B fast bowler, who was making his debut, was not advised that the game was due to start at 11 a.m. He eventually turned up at noon, to find that his team were fielding.

Under the rules of play he wasn't allowed to bowl for an hour because he had been off the field for that amount of time. The other fast bowlers toiled away in the heat and put in maximum effort.

Lunch arrived at 1 p.m. and play resumed at 1.40 p.m. The captain tossed the ball to the late arrival, telling him that it was his turn to bowl. The bowler tossed the ball back to his captain and said, 'Sorry, captain, I can't bowl now because I need half an hour for my lunch to settle.'

a *sour* note

Mike Denness, who captained the unsuccessful English team in the 1975 Ashes series against Australia, received an envelope addressed simply to: M. Denness, Cricketer.

Inside was the following brief note: 'If this letter finds you, then the postman thinks more of you than I do.'

the *earth* moves

Harry Seacombe is a great entertainer who has also played cricket. When describing his cricketing experiences he said, 'I'm the only person for whom a wide is called before the ball has been bowled. My shirt is used for the sightscreen. I'm used as a roller between innings. When I run between the wickets with Colin Milburn, we register seven on the Richter scale.'

yes, my lord

Hampshire were playing Warwickshire in a County Championship match at Bournemouth. Hampshire, who were being captained by Lord Lionel Tennyson, were being soundly beaten by Warwicks, who had made 545 for five.

Hants were out for 130 and, at 5.30 p.m. on the second day, were 150 for eight. They were resigned to the fact that they couldn't see the day out and there was still the next day to go.

At teatime, Hants were practising their golf swings in their dressing room. Tennyson said to the No. 11 batsman, 'Herman, at the fall of the ninth wicket, you'll appeal against the light when you get to the crease.'

When the ninth wicket fell, Herman strode to the crease as the sun shone brightly. There was still 20 minutes of play remaining before stumps and Herman knew that there was little chance of surviving. He was often referred to as the James Bond of cricket because he had a batting average of .007 and a highest score of seven.

Herman passed Tennyson, who said, 'Herman, remember what I told you?'

Herman replied, 'Yes, my lord. I can hear you but I can't see you.'

the *great* boycott

I bowled against many wonderful batsmen in my 20-year career —
players such as Viv Richards, Clive Lloyd, Desmond Haynes,
Gordon Greenidge, the Chappell brothers, Allan Border, Sunil
Gavaskar and David Gower, to name just a few — but Geoff Boycott,
the Yorkshire and England opening batsman, stands out.

He was a craftsman, technically very efficient and with a magnificent concentration level. He could occupy the crease and grind out
run after run. Anyone who can score 151 first-class hundreds
throughout their career obviously knows how to handle a bat.

I enjoyed bowling to Boycs because it was always a good contest.
He would play at balls that he had to and let me go outside the off
stump, if I was bowling too wide. He would wear me and the other
bowlers down and eventually bat all day. He was somewhat dour in
his approach to the game, but very determined and single-minded.

There are many stories told about Boycs, which may be unfair, but
are nevertheless quite amusing. People acknowledge that Boycs also
had a sense of humour.

Here are a few Boycott one-liners:

Boycott is so mean that he only breathes in.

He's so mean that if he caught measles he'd pass them on to other
people — one at a time!'

Boycott is covered in love bites — all self inflicted.

If Boycs was dining with us tonight, he'd still be eating the soup as
we finish our sweets.

At 21, I was a raw, excited, long-haired rookie with a bit of
potential as a fast bowler. In New Zealand we played cricket as

amateurs; on my first tour of England, I wanted to make an impression against the professionals.

The first match of the New Zealand tour was against Yorkshire at Headingley, in Leeds. I bowled the first ball of the match to Boycs. It was a rank long-up that sat up nicely wide of the off stump, which he promptly dispatched to the boundary for four runs with a cut shot backward of point.

I was disappointed but I was somewhat aghast as he walked down the pitch, tapped the divot down with his bat, looked at me and said, 'The name's Boycott, laddie, and you'll be seeing a lot of me during this test series.'

Three balls later I got one that pitched right on middle stump. He did everything correctly, got in behind it and looked to play it defensively. The ball moved away off the seam. He missed it and the off stump cartwheeled out of the ground.

I said, 'The name's Hadlee, so bugger off, you bastard!'

WEST INDIES

rolling on

A good pitch is rolled for weeks to get it flat and even. The captains are always interested in knowing something about the particular preparation a pitch has been given because winning the toss and deciding who would benefit most from batting or fielding first can be a match-winning decision.

The ground at Antigua, which is beside the prison, is maintained and looked after by the local prisoners. England were due to play a match there and the English captain, Tony Greig, while inspecting the pitch, started to talk to the person he thought was the grounds-man.

Tony asked him how long he had been rolling the pitch. The man replied, 'I've been rolling it for 10 years and I still have 10 years to go.'

Not quite the answer that Tony was expecting!

n o-balls

West Indian import, Junior Williams, had his troubles in New Zealand. A tall, fast bowler, he was having a great deal of difficulty with no-balls; he must have been bowling at least 10 per innings. He wasn't too impressed about the foot-fault calling or, for that matter, the number of times the umpires rejected his LBW appeals.

In utter frustration he said to umpire Steve Woodward, 'How come you can see the no-balls, man, but not the LBWs?'

'Because,' replied Steve, 'the no-balls are a lot closer.'

the *chosen* one

During our 1985 tour of the West Indies, the batting form of several players left a lot to be desired. Our coach, Frank Cameron (also the chairman of selectors), pulled aside Ken Rutherford, who had experienced a nightmare start to his test career with scores of nought, nought, four, nought, two, one and five — 12 runs at an average of 1.71.

Frank said to Ken, 'Tomorrow's test is going to be tough. The West Indian bowlers bowl even faster in front of their home crowds. I want to talk to you because I need a batsman with great concentration, a good eye, a strong constitution and who can really stand up to fast bowling. So that's why I'm making you 12th man.'

call me *amby*

Curtly Ambrose, a tall West Indian fast bowler, is feared all around the world. He has been an outstanding and effective fast bowler in all types of conditions because he has control of his pace and skill. He gets the ball to bounce, often disconcertingly, just short of a length on most pitches, causing very good batsmen all sorts of problems. He can certainly intimidate batsmen with some very useful bouncers.

When asked what his nickname was, he replied, 'They call me "Amby".'

'Is that short for Ambrose?'

'No mon, it's short for ambulance!'

lara rules

Many people say that Brian Lara, the diminutive West Indian left-hander, will be the next Bradman. It is hard to believe that anyone could be better than the Don, who was a legend in the game of cricket, a master batsman with a test average of 99.94 runs per innings. That average will never be surpassed. If a batsman averages 50-plus in test cricket today, over, say, 50 tests, he is regarded then as a great player.

The Don was asked how many runs he would have scored against the English attack of Angus Fraser, Andrew Caddick, Chris Lewis, Phil Tuffnell and Graham Hick. Bradman said, 'I'd have scored 50 or 60.'

The interviewer, somewhat surprised by Bradman's answer said, 'You averaged 99.94 runs per test innings but you'd only score 50 or 60 against that Pommie attack?'

Bradman replied, somewhat ruefully, 'Oh yes, but I'm 85 years of age at the moment!'

wally prepares

New Zealand played the West Indies in the 1979 World Cup at
Trentbridge in Nottingham. Wally Lees, New Zealand's wicket
keeper, was a little timid of fast bowlers — and who isn't?

Wally took all possible precautions to protect himself. He tucked
shin pads into his socks, wrapped towels around his legs and placed
his pads carefully over the top. Then he put his slip-in box into his
athletic support and wrapped his tie-on box over the top (double
protection). Next he wrapped a towel around his waist, put on his
chest protector, positioned his elbow guard, placed his helmet on his
head — and set off to face the Big Bird, Joel Garner.

Wally was hit on the foot first ball and a toe was broken. He was
also given out LBW for nought.

optimism

What's the definition of optimism in cricket?

Any batsman putting zinc ointment on his nose when he's going out to face the West Indian pace attack.

INDIA *and* PAKISTAN

Blowin' *in the* wind

Indian umpires have been called a lot of things in the past and I can see why. In the third test at Madras in 1976, I bowled to Anshuman Gaekwad, who took evasive action from a bouncer that never really took off. The ball didn't bounce much at all, Gaekwad lost his balance and the ball went through to keeper Wally Lees. Noticing that a bail had fallen off the wicket, we all appealed for the batsman to be given out, hit wicket. Glenn Turner was adamant that Gaekwad had knocked the bails off. The umpires conferred and gave him not out.

When we challenged the decision, the umpires said that the wind had blown the bails off. We couldn't believe it. It was a windless day and, even if there was the slightest breeze, the bail had fallen off on the wrong side of the wicket.

I was still fuming at the end of the over and mumbled a few naughty words as I snatched my hat out of the umpire's hand. The umpire then went over to the captain, Glenn Turner, and asked him to control his player. Turner replied, 'Once he starts whacking you over the head with it — that's when you'd better start worrying!'

Eventually, I knocked Gaekwad's off stump out of the ground and it was broken in two pieces. Somebody said, 'Bloody strong wind!'

With a great deal of delight, I picked up the pieces and ran off the field, even beating Gaekwad to the pavilion. I put both pieces in my bag as a souvenir. After inspecting the wicket I noticed the borer in it!

audience participation

Sunil Gavaskar, the Indian captain, didn't have a happy test series in New Zealand during their 1981 tour. In the second test at Christchurch, he had batted for three and a half hours and although he had scored only 53, he had been playing and missing the ball repeatedly. This was frustrating not only for the bowlers, but also for the crowd.

Someone in the No. 5 stand yelled out, 'Bowl him a piano and see if he can play that!'

'How the hell did your mother get you out?' was another call.

which way is the pitch?

Sarfraz Nawaz, Pakistan's big fast bowler, had an interesting sense of humour. In an ODI at Christchurch in 1973, New Zealand batted in brilliant sunshine in front of 12,000 people, scoring 187 from 38.3 overs. The light deteriorated very badly as the Pakistan innings progressed.

When Sarfraz came out to bat, it was very dark and, under normal circumstances, play would have been halted. As he walked out of the players' tunnel, he walked towards the No. 3 stand, which was on his left at a 90-degree angle. He pretended that he couldn't see the pitch, much to the delight of the crowd and even our players. He had the last laugh, however, as he proceeded to hit me for three consecutive fours as soon as he arrived at the crease.

doctor's *orders*

Most cricketers who tour India and Pakistan will suffer from diarrhoea, the 'shits', at some time or another. Danny Morrison had this problem during New Zealand's 1988 tour of India. Our team doctor gave him six suppositories and told him to use three a day for two days and then come back and see him again.

DK, who had never seen these things before, ate the first one and nothing happened. He ate the second and third and still nothing happened. He ended the day eating all six. He went back to the doctor, who asked him if he'd used all the suppositories. DK said that he'd taken all of them that day and nothing had happened.

The doctor said, 'What do you mean you've used all six today? Did you eat them or something?'

'What did you expect me to do with them?' DK replied. 'Stick them up my arse?'

spare *seat*

There are more than 800 million people living in India. A high percentage are cricket lovers and many of them are fanatical about the game. They turn up in their thousands to watch, support and cheer on their heroes. It's a rare sight to see any empty seats in the stadiums. When we played in Bombay at the Wankhede Stadium the gates closed an hour before play was due to commence. The stadium was absolutely packed except for one empty seat outside the players' viewing area.

When I asked an Indian gentleman why the seat was vacant, he replied, 'It is my wife's seat, but she passed away recently.'

'I'm sorry to hear that,' I said. 'Surely you have a friend who could use the seat?'

The man replied, 'Oh yes, sir, I have, but all my friends are at my wife's funeral.'

the *missing* wallet

Bob Cunis, a medium pace bowler who served New Zealand cricket well during the 1960s and early 1970s, was our coach on the 1988 tour of India. He's a fairly laid-back sort of character who enjoys a drink and a fag. Bob knows the game well and is very good with young pace bowlers.

While we were playing in Hyderabad, Bob lost his wallet. He thought that he had left it in his room but couldn't find it when he went back to look. The management of the hotel were called and the staff questioned. The wallet was eventually found in the foyer of the hotel, where it had fallen out of his bag. It was given to Danny Morrison, who in turn passed it on to Bob. End of story.

No. At 8.30 the next morning, Bob received a telephone call from a Detective Sergeant Singh. 'Mr Cunis, I am very sorry. We cannot find your wallet. We were most wanting to find it for you.'

Bob told him that everything was okay and his wallet had been found, intact.

'Oh Mr Cunis,' continued Detective Sergeant Singh, 'we are so pleased but we need you to sign a statement.'

'Everything's all right,' Bob repeated. 'I don't need to sign any statement.'

'Oh Mr Cunis, you don't understand. We are holding five people in jail on suspicion of theft,' said the policeman.

Bob was horrified. 'You must let them go! They're all innocent.'

The detective sergeant told Bob that they would be sending a Sergeant Patel around to the ground at 9.30 a.m. with a statement for him to sign.

We arrived at the ground around 9 a.m. and were standing in a circle doing some stretching when we noticed Bob talking to an Indian policeman. As Bob walked over towards us he was waving his arms and ranting and raving. He looked very brassed off.

When he joined us, we politely asked him what the problem was. Bob said, 'These blokes won't leave me alone and I'm getting bloody annoyed with all their carry-on!'

John Wright said, 'Did Detective Sergeant Singh have an accent?'

Bob answered, 'Of course he did, Wrighty . . . you bastard, Wrighty, you've set me up!'

Everyone broke up, including the policeman we had primed and who was still lurking, trying to piece the jigsaw together.

early bird

After five weeks on the Indian sub-continent during the 1996 World Cup I was growing used to expecting the unexpected.

On match days the commentary team was usually picked up from the hotel by 7.30 a.m. One morning in Faisalabad, I had fortunately woken at 6.30, as my requested 6.15 wake-up call had not eventuated.

I was sitting in the restaurant having a quick breakfast when at 7.25 a.m., just five minutes before we were due to leave for the ground, a porter came into the room carrying a chalkboard bearing the message: 'Mr Hadlee, please phone reception as there is a phone call for you'.

I did so and the voice at the other end said, 'Mr Hadlee, good morning, sir. This is your early morning wake-up call.'

everything's *all* right

There wasn't a lot to do on non-match days during the 1996 World Cup so I tended to stay in my room and watch the in-house videos. These two-hour films often took up to four hours to view because of the numerous power failures and the rewindings that these caused. But as annoying as this was, it wasn't as bad as the phone calls that came regularly throughout the day.

The phone would ring and I would say, 'Hello.'

'Sir Hadlee?'

'Yes, who is this?'

'I'm guest customer relations.'

'Yes, what do you want?'

'I'm wanting to know if everything's all right. Is there anything we can do for you?'

'No, I'm fine, thank you. Goodbye.'

These calls came at least three times a day for a week and I constantly bit my tongue to stop myself telling the woman exactly what I was thinking. Finally, though, I'd had enough.

'Hello.'

'Sir Hadlee, this is customer guest relations.'

'Why do keep ringing me?'

'It's my job to make our guests' stay more enjoyable. Is there anything I can do for you?'

'Yes, as a matter of fact there is. Can you stop ringing me?'

I didn't hear from her again and the stay was a little more pleasant from then on.

AUSTRALIA

saved!

In the first test against Australia at the MCG on the 1973-74 tour, we performed very badly and lost. The boundaries at the Melbourne cricket ground are very big — 90 metres or more — and on one occasion, David O'Sullivan had a long chase to the boundary to save a four.

Daffy Duck, as he is known, is not the quickest of movers. He 'waddled' at his usual pace in pursuit of this ball and dived to save an almost certain boundary. He gathered the ball as quickly as he could and fired his return to the keeper. I caught the ball some 40 metres from the wicket and threw it to the keeper, Ken Wadsworth.

Daffy smiled and said, 'Gee, they must have only run three. I must have run more quickly than I thought!'

Daffy was then startled to hear Ken say that they had run five! With all that effort, the Duck should have let the ball go for four.

pascoe's promise

Len Pascoe, the Australian fast bowler, is a great competitor and has served his country well. At times he can be very dangerous with his speed and accuracy but he has also been known to use verbal abuse and to bowl persistently short to batsman with the intention of causing injury. I've certainly enjoyed some of his comments to the batsmen.

On an historic occasion at Trentbridge in 1980, Notts defeated Australia by an innings. Lenny, known as Loosehead Len, had become so frustrated at beating the bat and being nicked through the slips for a series of fours, that he said, 'I'm going to get you! I can see blood. I'm calling for the ambulance!'

On another occasion during the same game, Roy Dexter was batting away very well and then he received a short ball from Loosehead, which hit him on the chest. Roy, who is a big lad, didn't bother rubbing the spot and the ball landed just in front of him. Loosehead said, 'Top guts, mate, top guts.'

As he was walking back to his bowling mark, he turned to Ashley Mallet and said, 'In my youth, he'd have gone down, but I'm an old man now and that's why he's still standing.'

bouncers

The Australian fast bowlers, in particular, are renowned for bowling bouncers and intimidating batsmen. Lenny Pascoe, after bowling a few bouncers, said to the umpire, 'Good ball, that. Did you see him change colour?'

'Good ball!' said the umpire. 'It would have been if you'd been bowling from the other end.'

Lenny couldn't say too much then.

much too *appealing*

The Aussies generally appeal for anything and everything to try and get an affirmative decision from the umpire. Lenny Pascoe, who was being particularly demanding during one game, was annoying the umpire with his excessive appeals.

Finally, the umpire said, 'There's only one man who appeals more than you, Lenny!'

'Oh, who's that?'

'Doctor Barnardo!' replied the umpire.

amended rules *of* play

New Zealand's disappointing results against Australia during their 1993-94 tour of Australia caused some concern to supporters back home. A drawn first test was followed by a humiliating defeat in the second test in Hobart (the greatest test loss in the history of New Zealand cricket — a defeat by an innings and 222 runs). The poor form continued with a loss in the third test by yet another innings.

In the Benson & Hedges World Series Cricket one-day international competition, Australia were on top of the points table, having won their first two matches. New Zealand's victory over South Africa at Hobart started to turn the tour around.

An article which appeared in one of the New Zealand newspapers, summed up New Zealand's pre-Christmas form and suggested amending the rules of cricket to give us a better chance of competing! 'Since modern cricket could be considered to be an evolving game, a group of concerned (distraught?) Auckland fans got together and drew up some suggested amendments to the rules of play, specifically for games between New Zealand and Australia.'

Some of these amended rules were:

1. All Australian batsmen must retire after reaching 100. (This should restrict the Aussies to no more than 1000 runs per innings. We're getting sick of seeing the same faces all the time.)

2. Australia must open the batting with their bowlers. (Otherwise we don't get to bowl at them and they are always picking on our boys.)

3. Shane Warne's googlies and flippers are not permitted (provided, of course, the umpires can pick them; our batsmen surely cannot. The Australian TV commentators seem to pick them after the fifth replay).

4. When one Waugh brother is dismissed, both are out. (This is only fair because they're twins.)

5. Australian batsmen must show respect for New Zealand bowlers whether they bowl badly or not.

6. Anybody of any nationality, creed, colour or persuasion, who is even remotely aware of where New Zealand is, can be eligible to play for us and strengthen our team.

SOUTH AFRICA

heads *or* tails

Peter Burge was the international match referee for the Mandela quadrangular one-day series and for the test matches in South Africa in 1994-95. With four different teams competing, there were always going to be language difficulties, especially when it came to the toss and calling heads or tails.

Peter Burge made it quite clear: 'I have the coin that you'll toss with. One side has heads on it, the other side tails. By the way, I don't understand Urdu, Afrikaans, Maori, Singhalese or English. I want all you captains to call in Australian — okay, fellas?'

Salim Malik said, 'Oh, frigging hell — I'll call bloody heads then.'

down *to* size

During the 1994-95 quadrangular cricket tournament in South Africa, former Warwickshire medium pace bowler turned commentator Jack Bannister told a lovely story on air about capturing his 1000th first-class wicket in 1965. As the victim, New Zealander Bevan Congdon, walked back to the pavilion all Jack's team mates shook him by the hand and patted him on the back, congratulating him on his milestone.

Then Jack heard Terry Jarvis, the New Zealand opening batsman at the non-striker's end, go up to the umpire and ask what all the excitement was about. 'Is that the bowler's first wicket?' Terry enquired.

As Jack said, 'Some of us unknown cricketers need to be a little humble.'

ship *ahoy*

Jack Bannister was commenting on the dismissal of Steven Jack, a big, red-headed South African fast bowler who was batting with Jonty Rhodes, who is very quick when it comes to running between wickets.

'Steven Jack has played that ball well off his legs to deep backward square. There should only be a single but Jonty Rhodes has called for two and is coming back for a second as the return is on its way to the keeper. Rhodes stops and goes back to the bowler's end, but Jack looks stranded. He turned and goes back to the keeper's end and he's run out by 10 metres. He should have made his ground — even the Queen Mary would have turned quicker than that.'

diving *for* cover

Clive Rice and I were commentating on the third test at Newlands, Cape Town, between New Zealand and South Africa.

'I've noticed, Clive,' I said at one point, ' that at the one-day games when it's rained and the covers are on the pitch, it's a temptation for one or more of the spectators to run onto the ground, dive onto the wet covers and see how far they can slide. It's called duck diving and security guards struggle to prevent it from happening.'

'Yes, Richard, I remember a male streaker in Durban running onto the ground and duck diving onto the covers. He slid for 25 metres, crashed his head into a pole and knocked himself out.'

I replied, 'So he was knocked on the head, so to speak.'

At that point I started to laugh. What the viewers could not hear was my producer's voice saying in my ear cans, 'There's one ball left.'

NOTTINGHAM

derek randall

You could write a book about Derek Randall. He's a talented batsman, a magnificent fielder and the sort of genuine character that the game of cricket needs. He was renowned for being predictable at the unpredictable!

We always felt that Arkle was a bit of a nutter and capable of doing the unbelievable or extraordinary at any time.

In the field, he had a habit of wandering all over the place and it wasn't uncommon for him to be many metres out of position. When Nottingham played Somerset at Taunton in 1984, Eddie Hemmings, our off-spinner, was bowling to Vic Marks and Derek, who had been positioned on the mid-wicket boundary, had wandered away some 30 metres and was at the deep mid-on boundary.

As Eddie started to bowl, he noticed Arkle out of position and called out, 'For goodness sake, Derek, get back to where you're supposed to be.'

Derek yelled back, 'It's all right, Eddie. I caught him here off your bowling two years ago!'

The captain, Clive Rice, then intervened and said, 'Derek, see that sign on the mid-wicket boundary that says "KP Nuts"? Stand in front of the word "Nuts" and don't move!'

Needless to say, the ball went in the air to wide mid-on and rolled over the rope for four runs.

Derek is never short of an answer, although there are times when the answer doesn't make much sense.

Notts won the County Championship in 1981 for the first time in 52 years. It was a moving and emotional experience, shared by all those at Trentbridge.

When a county team win the championships, it's traditional for them to play the first game of the next season at Lords against the MCC.

In April, 1982, a bitterly cold time of the year, we made the trip to Lords. The game was drifting along without much happening. If there was going to be any chance of a result, we had to encourage the MCC to be positive. We needed to give them quick runs so they would declare and give us a target on the third day. The best way to do that was to bowl someone who 'doesn't bowl'. Someone like Derek Randall.

He was instructed by Clive Rice to bowl anything and everything to allow the batsmen to score some runs. He was told to bowl six or seven overs and give away 60 or 70 runs. It was cashing-in time for the batsmen, great for starting the season and perhaps getting a big not out, which would help their average.

After four overs, Randall had three for 15. He had completely buggered up the game and had test players David Gower, Roland Butcher and Jack Richards all back in the pavilion.

The five front-line Nottingham bowlers — Mike Hendrick, Kevin Cooper, Clive Rice, Eddie Hemmings and I — were wicketless, while Randall walked off the Lords cricket ground to a standing ovation! After that performance, he was top of the first-class bowling averages for the season and there were five bowlers not too happy with that situation.

We all told Ricey that we weren't happy and felt that Randall had to bowl again that season to give a more accurate picture. We wanted to see him take his wickets at an expected average for Derek of around 70 to 80 runs each.

Derek got to hear about this and asked who we were playing in the next game. When he was told it was Lancashire at Old Trafford, he said, 'Oh, by gum! If I have to bowl at that 'ere Clive Lloyd, the field better scatter! Put one in Oldham, one in Preston, and the rest in Manchester City somewhere!'

Derek Randall showed yet again how quick he is with verbal responses, in a match at Notts during 1983, his benefit or testimonial year. (He had another, in 1993.)

Part of the benefit programme is to play some charity/celebrity matches at local grounds. The clubs are always keen to host these matches because they lift the club's profile and profits and the locals also get to see some of their heroes at close range.

During a charity match, Derek opened the batting with Basher Hassan. When he arrived at the crease, he was rather amazed to see that the umpire was a woman. Derek always took his guard on two legs but appeared somewhat distracted.

The umpire inquired, 'Do you want two legs or what?'

Derek looked up, a little surprised, and said, with a smile, 'I'd rather have what, but I suppose I'd better have the two legs first!'

Derek Randall had a great history for being involved in run out decisions. More often than not, it was his partner who suffered. Before he went out to bat, he practised his calling in front of the mirror: 'Yes, no, wait, oops, sorry!'

Notts travelled to Lords to play Middlesex. We batted first and Derek was in fine form, hitting the ball to all sections of the boundary. He raced away to 80, but unfortunately ran three of his team mates out in the process.

In the dressing room we waited for Arkle to return so that we could give him a bit of a blast. He arrived back and before we could get a word out, he said, 'Sorry fellas, I've been batting like Wally Hammond, but calling like Charlie Chaplin.'

Most cricketers who tour India and Pakistan have suffered from dysentery, stomach ailments and so on. Derek Randall was no exception. He was on the golf course ready to tee off when he disappeared behind some bushes, obviously to relieve himself.

Then came a bellow: 'Has anyone got any toilet paper?'

'No,' was the reply, 'but for goodness sake hurry up, Arkle, there are people waiting to tee off behind us.'

'Has anyone got any newspaper?'

Again, 'No,' was the reply.

'Has anyone got change for a 10 pound note?'

In the 1982 test series England v. India, Derek Randall was recalled to the England team after a four-year absence. In the first test at Lords he scored a magnificent 120-odd.

At the end of the day's play, tired but very happy, he returned immediately to his hotel to rest up. When he arrived back at his room, he tried to open the door with his key but he couldn't get it open. He was starting to get very irritated with the situation and decided to complain to the manager.

He said, 'This bloody door won't open!', to which the manager replied, 'I'm not at all surprised, sir. You're in the wrong hotel!'

hendrick's *humour*

Mike Hendrick, the former English seam bowler, was great entertainment value in our Notts dressing room.

He once told us about a charity match he played in. His wife, Cathy, accompanied him to most of his games and was there on this occasion. Invariably, Hendo would score a duck but as he fancied himself getting a few in this particular benefit match, he was promoted in the batting order. Unfortunately, he got out first ball so he went over and joined his wife to watch the rest of the game.

'Light all right?' she asked.

'Yes, perfect,' said Hendo.

'The wicket playing well?' asked Cathy.

'Oh, one of the best I've batted on,' Hendo replied.

'Well,' said Cathy, 'why are you out?'

'Well, my love,' he said, 'when I got out to the middle, I looked over to you and I couldn't bear seeing you all alone, so, here I am.'

the *right* thing *to say*

My Notts team mate, wicketkeeper Bruce French, was selected to play for England in the first test against New Zealand at Lords during our 1986 tour. I was still bowling when he came out to bat. Within several balls, I bounced him and, unfortunately, he ducked into the ball which hit him on the helmet. Bruce fell to the ground and had to be stretchered off.

Fortunately he was okay, but an x-ray showed that he had sustained a slight fracture. The next day I saw Frenchy, who was still a little dazed and took no further part in the match. When I saw his wife, Ellen, I expressed my regret at what had happened. It could have been much more serious, even fatal, had he not been wearing a helmet.

I was getting lost for words when Ellen suddenly said, 'Oh, don't worry. I've been wanting to do that to him for years!'

a *matter* of pace

Tim, Chop, Robinson was describing the pace at which India's Madan Lal bowled. 'He runs in a lot faster than he bowls. If he had more of a follow through, the ball would hit him on the back of the head.'

seeing *the* light

Notts played Essex at Trentbridge in 1948 and Essex, who batted first, made around 300. The two Notts openers, Walter Keaton and Charlie Harris, had to bat for the last half-hour of the day, in rather appalling and gloomy light. As Harris walked to the wicket, he called to the umpire, 'Where are you?'

'I'm over here.'

'Keep talking and then we should make contact,' said Harris.

Charlie, asking for a guard, said, 'Hang on a minute. I'll get my torch out so that you can see where my bat is!'

The Essex opening bowler ran in to bowl, but before he delivered the ball, Charlie stopped play and said to the umpire, 'Would you mind getting those lights in the dressing room turned off? They're blinding me.'

Needless to say, three minutes later they came off the field for bad light.

keith pont travels *in the* outfield

When Keith Pont joined the Essex staff as a youngster, many years ago, it was traditional for new players to patrol the boundary and do the running. He was sent by the captain to the third man position. At the end of the over, he was sent to the same position at the other end of the ground.

Ponty, getting fed up with all this travelling, found a bike and promptly used it to get from one end of the ground to the other.

no-ball, *no* laughing matter

One of the funniest things that I have seen on a cricket field happened at Trentbridge in 1981. Notts were playing Yorkshire in a 40-over Sunday League match. Pete Hacker, known as Reb (short for Rebel), had opened the bowling and didn't bowl too well. He had conceded 20 runs in four overs and the small Yorkshire crowd on the boundary started to give him a hard time.

Reb was relieved from bowling duties and was fielding at the deep mid-off position when Noddy Bore, our left arm spinner, bowled. Graham Stevenson, a hard-hitting batsman, hit a high catch to Reb, who stood under the ball and caught it. He turned to the Yorkshire crowd, who were 15 metres away, and raised the ball to them in one hand, then the other and then in both. The crowd went mad and beckoned him over to the boundary.

Meantime, Stevo and Bluey Bairstow, the other batsman, were running their third run, because the umpire had called 'no-ball'. The two batsmen were nearly falling over their bats with laughter as they kept running. Derek Randall was lying on the ground with his feet in the air, laughing himself stupid.

Although important runs had been given away, I must admit that even the captain, Clive Rice, had a sense of humour on this occasion. Noddy Bore, who hates conceding a run off his bowling, raised a cheek in a gesture that could have been taken as a smile!

HISTORY

strange *but* true

Many unusual things have happened in the fascinating history of cricket.

For example, bowlers have swung the ball so viciously that batsmen have changed hands to counteract the movement. Some bowlers have completed an over by bowling some balls right-handed and the others left-handed.

The game has been interrupted by rain, snow, hail, bad light, eclipses, pitches being dug up, floods and so on.

Other stoppages have been caused by animals. Dogs have wandered onto the field. Bees have stopped play. Snakes have slithered across the pitch. A runaway horse and cart has appeared on the ground. An ostrich has swallowed the ball; a cow has done the same.

Many games have finished early and some teams have decided to give the spectators their money's worth by playing a new game.

cricket was once played on horseback

In 1877, Gloucester batted with broomsticks and scored just under 300, while the Cheltenham team played with normal bats and had scored 50 for two by the end of the day's play.

In 1878, a ball was hit over a cliff and the umpire refused to call 'lost ball', so the batsmen went on to complete 264 runs while the ball was retrieved.

In the 1880s, a ball was hit down a steep slope and, while the fielders relayed the ball back to the wicketkeeper, the batsmen scored the necessary 46 runs to win the match off the first ball of the innings. (The fielders kept dropping the ball, which then rolled back down the slope.)

One bowler claimed to have dismissed three batsmen with one ball. He broke the thumb of the first victim with a fast rising ball and there was blood everywhere. His partner fainted and was carried off and the next batsman refused to bat.

Some bowlers are instructed, for tactical reasons, to bowl a load of rubbish to allow the batting team to score easy and extra runs to force a declaration. In 1936, J.H. Human bowled a maiden over, but conceded 24 runs. He bowled six deliberate wides that beat the wicketkeeper and went to the boundary each time for four.

In 1796, a team of pensioners, each with only one leg, played a team, each of whom had only one arm. The one-legged team won by 111 runs, but they suffered several casualties in the process. There were five broken legs, all wooden, with four of them breaking when they were running. One batsman came out to bat with his wooden leg in the shape of a cricket bat. (There was probably no chance that he could be given out LBW!)

all over

Some test careers have been over just as quickly as they started. In 1924, J.C.W. MacBryan was selected for England to play against the Springboks. The game was rain affected and he neither bowled nor batted. He was never selected again.

IT HAPPENED *to* ME

a *bowler's* graveyard

I've been fortunate enough to have played cricket all around the world. Some of the pitches I've bowled on have been very flat, low, slow and docile and, as a fast bowler, they've almost broken my heart.

In India and Pakistan, this type of pitch is common and therefore you prepare yourself accordingly. But to have pitches like this in New Zealand is unbelievable. In a country like ours with plenty of rain and sunshine, the grass should grow well. Many Kiwi grounds-men kill pitches because of poor preparation or a lack of knowledge.

I played in a game at Trafalgar Park, in Nelson, and as usual I inspected the wicket before the match and found that there wasn't a blade of grass on it. I was naturally disappointed, because it meant only one thing: a batsman's paradise and a bowler's graveyard — which proved to be the case.

I was standing in the loo, relieving myself of excess weight, when someone standing alongside me asked me what I thought about the pitch.

I replied, 'It's a bloody disgrace and it does the game of cricket a disservice. There were only three blades of grass on that pitch and they were behind the wickets. After the first over, the umpire had stood on those blades and killed them!'

The person I was speaking to was the groundsman.

Gotcha!

Peter Roebuck is a sincere and respected cricket writer with many interesting thoughts. Once, however, he wrote a newspaper article about me that I felt amounted to character assassination — he called me austere, morose, selfish, said I was a bad influence on the team and that I lacked a sense of humour. It hurt to see this in black and white, even if it was true! The real point was that he was criticising a fellow player while he was still playing the game himself.

I didn't say anything to him as I knew we would meet on the pitch when I returned to England the following year — he was the opening batsman for Somerset and I was the opening bowler for Nottinghamshire.

In August that year Somerset came to Trentbridge. The pitch was ideal for me — hard, fast, green and bouncy. Clive Rice won the toss and I suggested we bowl first. 'Let's use the conditions to our favour,' I said. 'I'm feeling really good and I've got a debt to square with Roebuck.'

I picked exactly the ball I wanted, I had magnificent rhythm, I bowled beautifully — with speed and accuracy. I beat Roebuck four times outside the off stump with superb outswingers and wicket-keeper Bruce French took the ball.

'Great,' I said to myself. 'He's mine. It's only a matter of time. I'm going to show him a thing or two!'

With the first ball of the next over I found the edge of his bat with a beauty that pitched, bounced and left him late. Clive Rice, standing at first slip, dropped him. 'Bugger it!' I said (or words to that effect).

I proceeded to hit Roebuck on the pads, on the box, in the chest, I broke a finger and hit him on the helmet. 'Great, got him!' I said.

Six and a half hours later, he was 221 not out!

I guess it goes to prove that if you lose control and try too hard for the wrong reasons, you come off second best. (Revenge did come weeks later when I had him LBW first ball for nought in a Sunday League match at Taunton in Somerset.)

humour for *hadlee*

I've been called many things during my career, some pleasant, others not. As a player, however, one must accept the criticism and comments from the media, spectators and sometimes even from friends.

Some of the comments which have appealed to my sense of humour are:

Q. Why is Richard Hadlee like a gynaecologist among pygmies?

A. Because he keeps going in for those short-pitched deliveries.

Richard Hadlee is called a big thinker, but only by those who lisp.

Richard Hadlee is New Zealand's No.1 quickie. Picture him running in to bowl, arms swinging, legs pumping up and down, nostrils parted as he reaches that climatic moment of delivery. But what about his bowling?

Every time Hadlee opens the fridge door, he appeals against the light.

When there's a clap of thunder during an electrical storm, Hadlee takes a bow.

There are times when I'd like to kick Richard Hadlee in the teeth, but why should I improve his looks?

Hadlee never gets lost because everyone tells him where to go.

who **are** *you?*

Young kids are great autograph hunters, always thrusting their books, pieces of paper, photos and magazines in front of your nose, expecting you to sign all the time. On occasions, it's easy to get frustrated when pens don't work or they leak or when the top is still on the pen. Often, too, kids choose the wrong time to ask for an autograph.

I remember well the first time I played for Canterbury, replacing my brother, Dayle, in the 1971-72 season. The autograph hunters eventually came up to me and one little lad asked me to sign his book. In it I could see names like Brian Hastings (Canterbury), Bob Cunis, Ross Morgan and Hedley Howarth, all current Auckland or test players. I felt honoured to be in such great company when all of a sudden my confidence was shattered.

The little lad said, 'Who the hell are you?'

I said, 'I'm Richard Hadlee. I'm a new player on the scene.'

'Oh,' he said, 'I don't want your signature. Have you got a rubber?'

in *black* and *white*

The traditional annual cricket match at Luggate, near Wanaka, involves ex-cricketers (All Whites), playing ex-rugby players (All Blacks). In a relaxed environment, the match is played on an artificial surface, in front of approximately 1500-2000 spectators. Everyone gets to bat and bowl and there is always plenty of action, especially when you have Lance Cairns repeatedly hitting the ball out of the ground! (One year, Lance scored a 26-ball 88.)

The 1993 match was played in typical spirit. The All Whites, who always bat first, usually score around 360 or more off 40 overs. It was decided this year that we would try to get around 280, to make the game more competitive and allow the rugby players the chance to get near our score.

Cairnsy, who scored 70, buggered up the theory and we reached 342 off 40 overs. Jeff Crowe scored a nicely compiled 52 before he was bowled by a ball that he should have left alone.

The All Blacks were faced with a very difficult task. The only thing in their favour was that they always had an extra five overs to try and balance the game.

I bowled the first ball to ex-fullback Robbie Deans. Robbie, who had played some cricket at a representative level for Country Districts, charged me, hitting the ball over the top for six runs. This was an ominous sign for what was to follow as he reached 100.

Alan Hewson, another fullback, scored 70, Kieron Crowley, also an ex-fullback, used his attacking ability and looked very capable as he scored 40. (The All Blacks won the match quite easily with two overs to spare!)

Jeff Crowe, who has lost a fair percentage of his hair and looks remarkably bald from the front, took his turn at bowling. His first ball barely reached the wicket at the batsman's end. Ken Nicholson, a useful fast bowler in his time, was on the PA system and Jeff, running in to bowl his second delivery, stopped in his tracks when he heard: 'Jeff is waiting for the sun to reflect off the solar panel on his head to help him with some extra strength and pace!'

Two balls later, Crowley was bowled by a beauty which seamed back. As he walked back to the pavilion the PA system roared out: 'There must have been a break in the clouds!'

bowled *over*

On my last tour of India, in 1988, I was in search of my world record 374th wicket. It eventually came on the morning of the first test at Bangalore, when Arun Lal was caught by Chris Kuggeleijn at third slip.

Kapil Dev, who has been a wonderful performer for India over the years, is a great friend. While we were in Bombay, Kapil and I were asked to visit a hospital to meet and talk with terminally ill kids.

I asked Kapil, who was driving, if he was a good driver. 'Oh no, of course I'm not a good driver!' he replied, with a grin. On the way to the hospital, we were travelling at around 30 kilometres an hour because the roads were congested with cars, cows, carts and people.

All of a sudden, there was a thud on the bonnet and against the windscreen. A pedestrian had wandered in front of the car and ended up on it.

We were all quite shaken because this chap, who had been hit quite hard, had landed on the road and lay all curled up. We put him in the back of our car as we were heading for the hospital. After seeing the kids, Kapil and I returned to check on our accident victim, who appeared to be all right. The doctors advised us that he had several broken bones and would be in some pain when he sobered up.

I mentioned the incident to the lads later that night.

Although Chris Kuggeleijn appreciated that the whole incident was serious, he saw that it also had a humorous element to it. According to Chris, the guy we had knocked over would be able to boast about waiting for years to find Kapil and Hadlee driving together and, even with more than 700 test wickets between them, they still couldn't bowl him over!

from *sir* to *sir*

During the 1990 tour of England, I was awarded the finest accolade of my career — a knighthood for services to New Zealand cricket. I received a lovely letter from Sir Donald Bradman, congratulating me on the award and offering me a little advice on how it might change my lifestyle.

At the bottom of the letter was a little PS saying, 'Enclosed in the envelope is a cartoon which appeared in one of the Australian newspapers, honouring the occasion of your knighthood.'

The cartoon depicted me taking off into my run-up from the boundary edge. An Australian barracker — a short, rotund bloke with a beer gut, wearing a cowboy hat with corks dangling from the rim to keep the flies off — was sitting on the picket fence with a beer can in his hand. His T-shirt bore the inscription : 'You're a wanker, Hadlee.' The cartoon showed me turning around to the fellow saying, 'It's Sir Wanker to you, mate!'

To get this from the Don really tickled my fancy.

who needs *a* bat?

Gamesmanship or byplay is part of cricket — it always has been and always will be. During New Zealand's 1993-94 tour of Australia, Australia had competently outplayed New Zealand throughout the series with consistent batting, fine fielding and some outstanding bowling, especially by Shane Warne.

In the third test, Danny Morrison, New Zealand's fast bowler, came out to bat at No. 10, without his bat. He had conveniently forgotten to take it out with him because he felt he didn't need it, with scores in the series so far of nought, nought, nought, nought and 20 not out.

He played well in his last innings and, by using some good foot-work and technique, he perhaps showed the New Zealand batsmen how to combat Shane Warne, who had taken 18 wickets in the series.

fast, *faster*, fastest

In Perth, in 1979, the fastest bowlers in the world gathered to battle it out for the supreme title. Substantial prize money was offered, not only for the fastest bowling but for the most accurate: the bowler who hit the middle stump with the fastest delivery would win the award.

Players arrived from all over the world: Mike Procter from South Africa, Colin Croft, Andy Roberts and Michael Holding from the West Indies, Imran Khan and Sarfraz Nawaz from Pakistan, Dennis Lillee, Jeff Thomson and Lenny Pascoe from Australia, and myself from New Zealand.

After a loosening-up over, we were into the real thing. Because no extra balls were allowed and any no balls bowled didn't count, rhythm and timing were important. We were timed by a special camera that gave the precise speed of each delivery.

Jeff Thomson was by far the quickest bowler, being timed at nearly 100 miles per hour, and averaging 93 throughout his over. Michael Holding, Imran and Andy Roberts followed with speeds in the high 80s. Lillee, rather surprisingly, was timed in the mid-80s, as was I. Procter came ninth and poor old Sarfraz, with a speed in the high 70s, came last. 'They could have timed Sarfraz with a sun dial!' was one comment.

in *at the* death

The changes to the game over the last few years have ensured that cricket is becoming more popular with a wide variety of spectators who are keen to attend the games and support the local heroes.

Some people make all sorts of excuses to get out of work or school to watch the tests or ODI games. A friend of mine, who shall remain nameless, decided to get out of school and go down to Lancaster Park to watch the West Indies playing New Zealand. He advised his teacher that he had to go to his uncle's funeral and was therefore, given the afternoon off school.

As the match went on and the West Indies had progressed to 250 for no wicket, my young friend received a tap on the shoulder. He turned around to come face to face with his teacher. 'So this is your uncle's funeral!'

'Looks like it,' said the boy. 'He's the bowler.'

directions

In 1993, I had to drive from Preston to Bradford to attend the opening of a new Tesco shopping centre. When I arrived in Bradford, I was somewhat confused with the traffic directions so I decided to stop and ask directions. As it happened, the local I asked was an Indian gentleman. I said, 'I'm wanting Tesco.'

I guess he must have recognised me as he said, 'You are wanting Tesco? Ah yes! You are wanting test score! India 224 for two.'

all the *best* to border

The Gabba came alive on 19 December 1993, when 17,000 people turned up to acknowledge a true champion in Australian sport. Allan Border was not only the captain of the Australian cricket team, but also the most capped player in both test and one-day international cricket, and the leading run scorer in the history of the game. AB is also a national hero.

At times the quality of cricket in this tribute game was very impressive and the entertainment value was excellent, with many novel ideas being used by the cross-section of players, who included people from other sporting codes. Who would have thought that an umpire would agree to wearing a hat with a camera attached to it?

The batsmen and some of the fielders wore microphones, enabling the Channel 9 commentary team, consisting of Bill Lawry, Tony Greig and Richie Benaud, to ask them for comments on what was happening out in the middle.

For example, when I started batting, Tony Greig said, 'What's your plan out there, Paddles?' to which my reply, heard by television viewers in Australia and New Zealand, was, 'Hold on, Tony. I've just swallowed a fly! What's the question again?'

'Have you been given any instructions?' Tony asked.

'Yea,' I replied. 'The captain, Rod Marsh, has told me to get on with things and try to score 60 off 10 balls, but not to take any risks!'

During my rather quick-fire 44, which included several miscues along with some good ones, Bill Lawry asked me, while I was preparing for the next delivery from Alan Langer, where I intended to hit the following ball.

'Over mid-wicket for six, Bill,' I replied. I hit it well and said, 'That's six, Bill.'

Through my earpiece I heard a voice say, 'It's only going to be four, Sir Richard.'

Bugger it, I thought and when I noticed that the ball was going to pull up just short of the boundary, audiences on both sides of the Tasman would have heard me say, 'Oh shit! I'm going to have to run, Bill!'

There was plenty of nostalgia out there that day. I couldn't resist bowling an underarm delivery to Greg Chappell. For two overs I had ignored the crowd's calls to 'Give us an underarm, Hadlee' but suddenly it seemed like a good idea. Unfortunately, it went wider than I would have liked and Greg, who wasn't expecting it, reacted quite quickly, putting his foot to the ball and attempting to kick it in to the air and then swipe it over the boundary for six. Had I bowled it straighter, I would have had great delight in appealing for an LBW decision. Although Greg's timing wasn't quite right, he still managed to hit it for four.

EXTRAS

the *bobbitt* delivery

There are many types of deliveries bowled in the game of cricket. Some are potentially more dangerous than others, such as the 'Bobbitt' — it's short of a length, it's a dangerous, vicious and painful delivery, it's an off-cutter, it moves away in the air, it's difficult to score from and it's recommended that the cut and pull shots be avoided!

batting *in a* crisis

There seem to be very few big scores in the game of cricket today and some players are never happy with their performance.

In 1938, Arthur Wood, who batted at No. 8, went in when the score was 770 for six. He scored a quick 53 and put on 106 with Joe Hardstaff for the seventh wicket before getting out. The score was now 876 for seven. As he walked off, he turned to one of the members in the stands and said, 'Just like me to get out in a crisis.'

hit *on the* paddy

There's not much representative cricket played in Ireland, but when the national team actually plays the odd game against touring teams, they enjoy the occasion and the experience. A lot of cricket is played at the local level. During one game, the Royal Ulster Constabulary were playing the Metropolitan Police, in Belfast.

One of the RUC batsmen, Paddy O'Reilly, had been batting for hours and scored only one run. Every ball he faced produced the same result. A forward defensive prod at the ball for no runs, except the cover drive that had gone to fine leg for a single.

All of a sudden, Paddy missed one and was hit on the pad and given out LBW. 'Wouldn't have hit the stumps,' Paddy said to the umpire.

'I know,' the umpire replied.

'Then why am I out?' asked Paddy.

'Loitering with intent,' was the umpire's reply.

short and to the *point*

English commentator Jack Bannister is witty, organised, authorita-
tive, constructive and analytical. He also likes to tell cricket stories to
any one who's prepared to listen.

He told me the tale about John Emburey of Middlesex and
England playing in a benefit match which included players from
other sporting codes. Embers dismissed 5 foot 1 soccer striker Tony
Cottee for 10 and then got rid of a 5 foot TV personality first ball —
caught by Mike Gatting at point. Embers turned to Gatt and said,
'That's got rid of those two. Snow White must be due to bat soon.'

all in a day's play

Tony Cozier, the West Indian cricket commentator, was talking on live television about the performances of West Indian all rounder Winston Benjamin during his 1995 New Zealand tour.

He said, 'Winstone is a "daisy" player.'

'What does that mean, Tony?' I asked.

'Well, he's the type of player whose performance depends on the mood he's in at the time. Some days he does . . . some days he doesn't.'

get off the grass

Banners can be a lot of fun, but they can be painful reminders for any players who have been involved in misdemeanours. During the 1995 South African tour, three New Zealand players, Stephen Fleming, Matthew Hart and Dion Nash, admitted to smoking marijuana and were suspended for a couple of weeks and fined $250 each.

They missed the three ODIs against the West Indies, but a banner appeared at Eden Park: 'Watch out, West Indies, New Zealand are playing with no Hart, Fleming or Nash, rather no Hash'.

Someone in the crowd also produced a cigarette almost 2 metres long and carried it around the ground. It was inscribed with the words: 'New Zealand's secret weapon'.

you can bank *on it*

The centenary year of New Zealand cricket had not been a happy time. By the time of the Sri Lankan tour in 1995 we needed to win, to regain some sort of credibility in the eyes of the public. In Hamilton the Bank of New Zealand, which sponsors the international series, hosted both teams at a welcome cocktail party.

The Sri Lankan manager, Neil Perera, was invited to speak on behalf of his team. Having said that his team was looking forward to the tests and ODIs, he went on, 'I would like to acknowledge the support and sponsorship of the Bank of Sri Lanka here in New Zealand.' The sudden chuckle and murmur in the room made Neil realise what he'd said. He recovered brilliantly.

'I meant, of course, to say the Bank of New Zealand. In fact, the Bank of New Zealand should have a branch in Colombo and, if they did, I would guarantee at least 17 new accounts.'

too much *hot* air?

Ian Smith, the former New Zealand wicketkeeper, took up TV commentating when he retired from the game in the 1990s. Stockley has a bright and breezy approach to life and his commentary is quite refreshing. Part of his job is to present the weather forecast for the day's play.

Before the toss he would appear in a variety of situations to give his meteorological thoughts. It was always interesting to discover where he might appear next — on a tractor, a mower, a roller or in a stand.

When we were in Hamilton for a one-day match against Sri Lanka, Stockley was positioned in a hot air balloon, a few metres above the ground, but securely anchored by guide ropes. It was impressive to see this intrepid adventurer standing in his basket, his life dependent on the skill of others to keep him there. (There were one or two suggestions from his former team mates that the ropes should be cut.)

During his broadcast, there was a sudden whoosh of hot air, released to keep the balloon stable. Stockley continued, unfazed: 'and if Peter Sharp [a rather wordy commentator] was up here with me now, we would have no problems staying up here a little bit longer. However, the rest of the forecast today is for light showers with the odd burst of electrical thunderstorms, with vicious claps of thunder. Quite frankly, there's little likelihood of play today.'

who nose *what* to do

Most people know that Ken Rutherford, Ruds, has what could be described as an interesting facial feature. At a cricket function in Wellington he himself told the story about the game at the MCG during the 1993 one-day series against Australia, when big Craig McDermott was bowling. Ruds edged one to wicketkeeper Ian Healy. The Australians appealed for a caught behind and Ruds waited for the decision — not out, said umpire Steve Randall, to the displeasure of the other team.

David Boon, fielding in the bat/pad position, said to Ruds, 'Hey, listen here, Pinocchio, any more lies from you, and that nose of yours is going to get bigger and bigger.'

I laughed mightily at this, thinking that it took some doing on Ruds' part to take the Mickey out of himself in this way.

Ruds then caught sight of me in the front row. 'Hey Paddles,' he said, 'I wouldn't laugh if I was you. Looking at the size of your nose, you've been telling lies for 20 years.'

There wasn't much I could say after that!

a *dog's* tale

The fortunes of the New Zealand cricket team varied considerably during the 1995 centenary season. Some of the performances were very disappointing as we suffered loss after loss . . .

An avid supporter walked into the pub with his dog.

The barman said, 'That dog can't come in here. He must be kept outside.'

The cricket fan said, 'This is a good dog. He won't cause any harm while I have a quick drink.'

The barman somewhat reluctantly agreed to let the dog stay. The man ordered a pint of beer and asked for a drink for his dog. After the dog had finished his drink, he knocked the glass over with his tail and broke it. When the man finished his drink, the dog broke his glass as well.

The barman was very annoyed. 'I thought you said he was a good dog. What did he do that for?'

'Well, normally he is,' said the man, 'but sometimes he gets very frustrated and annoyed at the performances of the cricket team and he's got to take it out on someone or something.'

'What if the team wins? What does he do then?' asked the barman.

'Oh, I don't know,' said the cricket supporter, 'I've only had him for four years.'

leave it to *liz*

Ian Gunner Gould was a very useful wicketkeeper for Surrey, Middlesex and England, especially in one-day cricket. During the English tour of New Zealand in 1983 Gunner replaced Bob Taylor, England's No. 1 keeper, at the ODI in Christchurch.

Gunner dropped Bruce Edgar in the first over and generally had a disappointing day behind the stumps. Things didn't improve when he batted — out for nought in the first over.

At the post-game press conference Gunner was asked, 'Do you think Bob Taylor would have performed better than you today?'

Gunner stared at the reporter with a surprised look that quickly turned into a smile and replied, 'Even Elizabeth Taylor would have performed better than me today.'

just *five* more

Ray Julian umpired English county cricket during the 10 years I spent there playing for Notts in the 1980s. He was a very likeable chap who took great delight in keeping his personal tally of victims. At any time, he could tell you his count to date of the LBW, caught, stumped and run-outs he'd given.

One day at Trentbridge I went into the umpires' room to select the ball I wanted for that day's play and Ray asked, 'What end are you bowling from today, Paddles?'

I replied, 'I'll wait until I get out in the middle and see which way the wind's blowing.'

'I think you should bowl from the Ratcliffe Road end,' said Ray.

'We'll see.'

As I walked onto the field, I could see Ray holding his handkerchief in the air to see which way the breeze was blowing. Then I heard him say to his fellow umpire, Jack Hampshire, 'Jack, do you mind if I stand at the Ratcliffe Road end today? I think I'll get a few more today with the way Paddles has been bowling this season. I need five more for me 100 this season — if Paddles bowls straight, there are at least four LBWs and a caught behind.'

I marked my run-up from Ray's end and took six for 38 in that innings, leaving Ray one short of his target. But he got it in the first over when we batted.

happy to go

Harold Larwood, Lol, the famous fast bowler of the 1920s and 1930s, also played for Notts. Batsmen all over England feared his pace and aggression.

Lol once let one go at the Leicestershire opening batsman, and the ball flew past his nose. The next ball hit him on the upper body, the third gloved him and sailed over the gully for four runs, the fourth found the outside edge of the bat and went through to the fielder at first slip.

Satisfied that the ball had carried and the catch had been fairly held, the batsman started to walk back to the pavilion. But the fielder, lying on the ground, said, 'I didn't catch the ball. It bounced in front of me — it was a bump ball.'

The batsman kept walking but turned to say, 'It was a fair catch all right — it was close enough for me. I'm more than happy to go. I've got a wife and two kids to look after.'

members

A hooded streaker ran through the women's changing room at the local cricket grounds. Four women were there at the time and all were most unimpressed. Three said, 'It isn't my husband.' The fourth woman said, 'And he isn't even a member of the club.'

a *call* from above

One day well-known cricket commentator Rex Alston read in the Times that he had died — there was a beautiful tribute by the editor. He rang this gentleman and said, 'It's Rex Alston speaking. I note with interest my untimely death. I'd like to thank you for the lovely obituary.'

There was a long pause on the other end of the phone and then a very quiet voice said, 'And where are you calling from, Mr Alston?'

the unkindest *cut* of all

One day English cricketer Patsy Hendren was travelling by train from Manchester to London when he noticed another cricketer sitting in the same compartment. The other man was still dressed in his whites but had a red scarf around his neck.

'Been playing cricket, lad?' asked Patsy.

'Yes,' came the reply in quiet whisper.

'How did you get on?' enquired Patsy.

'Oh, I had a shocking day,' was the answer. 'I got no wickets for 87 runs, I dropped three catches and I was run out second ball.'

'Good God!' cried Patsy, 'if that had happened to me, I'd have cut my throat.'

'I just have.'

how big?

Joel Garner, the wonderful fast bowler from the West Indies who stood 6 feet 8 inches tall, had the amazing ability to get the ball to bounce sharply from a length. Once the Big Bird was asked whether other parts of his body (and one in particular) were in proportion to his tremendous height. 'If they were,' was the reply, 'I'd be 12 foot 6.'

an important *announcement*

All major cricket grounds have a public address system and throughout a day's play many messages and announcements are broadcast to the spectators.

Once when I was playing at the MCG an announcement came over the PA system. 'Mr Michael Mason, would you please go home. Your wife is in labour and she would like some transport to the hospital.'

A chuckle ran around the ground.

Twenty minutes later, there was another announcement. 'Mr Mason, would you please go home! Your wife now desperately needs to get to the hospital.'

Thirty minutes later there was another plea. Then finally, after another 25 minutes, the announcer said, in a rather bland and somewhat subdued voice, 'Mr Mason, would you please go the Mercy Hospital where you wife has just given birth to a 7-pound boy. Congratulations.'

how *many* balls?

The first ball I bowled in test cricket was a full toss and Sadiq Mohammad hit it behind square on the leg side for four. I had no idea then that 18 years and some 66,341 balls later, I would bowl my last ball in test cricket to the legendary English No. 11 Devon Malcolm, at Edgbaston on 9 July 1990. He was LBW for nought; in fact he faced six balls in the whole match. I bowled all of these and got him out twice for a pair. At the end of the match he came into our dressing room and asked me to sign his run chart.

caught *out*

On my last tour of India in 1988, I got the world record 374th test wicket to go past Ian Botham, but I was in search of many more.

When any No. 11 batsman comes out to bat there's an air of expectancy, but this was particularly the case when Indian player Narenda Hirwani strode to the crease. He struggled to hold the bat, let alone use it. On the flat docile Indian pitches, however, bowling to Hirwani became frustrating because, ball after ball, he kept planting that front foot of his down the pitch. He played at and missed a few, but I still felt he was mine — it was only a question of time.

At the end of one over I said to keeper Ian Smith, 'Stockley, I'll find the edge soon, so be ready for the catch.'

Smithy looked at me and said, 'Catches be buggered, Paddles. I'm going to stump this bloke.'

This knocked the stuffing out of me — as the No. 1 new ball strike bowler it would have been insulting for me to see the wicketkeeper standing up behind the stumps. Within a few balls I saw Stockley move up behind the stumps and Martin Crowe took a few steps forward from slip.

I thought to myself, 'Bugger this, these blokes are taking the mickey out of me. I think I'll slip one down the leg side and the ball might go for four byes and that won't impress the keeper.'

So I fired one down the leg side and Stockley's arm went out to his left at full stretch and in a flash the bails were whipped off, Hirwani was out, stumped, and I had another test wicket. Smithy walked up to me tossing the ball from hand to hand and said, 'And what's more, Paddles, that ball didn't even spin and that's impossible on this sort of pitch at your pace.'

champagne *all* round

Freddy Trueman was on the verge of being the first test bowler to capture 300 test wickets and therefore make cricketing history. England were playing Australia, so his record-breaking victim would have to be an Aussie, but which one?

Freddy became friendly with Aussie fast bowler Neil Hawke, who said, as fast bowlers often do, 'When I come out to bat, you look after me and when you bat, I'll look after you.'

Freddy thought about this and replied, 'Hawky, if you become my 300th test victim, I'll shout you a bottle of champagne.'

As it turned out, when Hawke arrived at the crease Freddy had 299 test wickets. Somehow Hawke got to 14 when Colin Cowdrey took a catch to give Freddy the 300 — a magical moment.

True to his word, Freddy shouted Neil Hawke a bottle of champagne. Later on his team mates said, 'Wasn't it a wonderful gesture by Harry Seacombe to send 12 bottles of champagne into the dressing room in honour of Fred's record!'

well fielded

I now qualify for the Golden Oldies cricket teams — the over 40s — for which the basic rule is that, if you practise during the week, you get dropped!

We now have a team called the Hadleonians, made up of family and friends. When we went overseas to play some games in England, we went first to the lovely county of Kent to play in Canterbury.

When a loose ball was on its way to the boundary, Ross Morgan, a sprightly fielder of 52 and a former New Zealand opener, chased hard. As the batsmen turned for four, the return came in, rocketing over the stumps and the bails were removed — a run out: one for 93. As we gathered to congratulate each other, I noticed that we were one player short.

Ross was still on the boundary, down on his hands and knees. The chase had obviously exhausted him. I went over and said, 'Well done, Roscoe — brilliant work and a wonderful throw. Well fielded.'

'Well fielded be buggered,' was the reply, 'I'm still looking for the ball. I've just run him out with an apple.'